CHAPTER 1

THE POWER OF THE OOZE

Have you ever felt the power of music? When your hands start clapping, your feet start tapping and there is nothing else in the world you can do but dance. Imagine that feeling. Hold it for a moment. Now, crank it up to a thousand!

This, my friends, is the power of the Ooze. The power of the Ooze is different for everyone. But everyone has it. We are all able to share in each other's, as long as others are willing to share it with you. And this band certainly is!

First, we have the bringer of the beat, Ricky Ignition. He's got more energy

©2024 BOOKLIFE PUBLISHING LTD.
KING'S LYNN, NORFOLK, PE30 4LS, UK

ISBN 978-1-80505-174-9

ALL RIGHTS RESERVED. PRINTED IN INDIA.
A CATALOGUE RECORD FOR THIS BOOK IS
AVAILABLE FROM THE BRITISH LIBRARY.

THE OOZE CREW AND THE GIG OF DOOM
WRITTEN BY E.C. ANDREWS
BASED ON A STORY BY NOAH LEATHERLAND
EDITED BY NOAH LEATHERLAND
ILLUSTRATION BY T MORRELL
BACKGROUND IMAGES COURTESY OF KLYAKSUN VIA SHUTTERSTOCK.COM

ABOUT THE AUTHORS
AFTER GRADUATING FROM HER MASTER'S DEGREE IN THE STUDY AND PERFORMANCE OF SHAKESPEARE, E.C. ANDREWS FOUND HER FOREVER HOME IN THE BOOKS AND STORIES THAT HAVE FILLED HER LIFE WITH WONDER FOR AS LONG AS SHE CAN REMEMBER. WISHING TO SHARE THAT WONDER WITH OTHERS, SHE HAS WORKED IN VARIOUS FACETS OF THE PUBLISHING INDUSTRY EVER SINCE, WRITING COMIC BOOKS, FILM REVIEWS, HISTORICAL DOCUMENTARIES, PROSE FICTION AND MORE.

NOAH IS A LIFELONG FAN OF COMIC BOOKS, VIDEO GAMES AND PRO WRESTLING. TRYING TO TAP INTO ALL THE THINGS THAT MAKE THESE HOBBIES COOL IS WHAT DRIVES NOAH'S WRITING. NOAH WAS A RELUCTANT READER AS A KID (AND STILL IS), SO HE HOPES TO PUT A BIT MORE FUN AND EXCITEMENT INTO CHILDREN'S BOOKS.

ABOUT THE ILLUSTRATOR
T HAS BEEN AN ARTIST SINCE THEY WERE 11 YEARS OLD, DREAMING OF BEING ABLE TO BRING STORIES TO LIFE. T HAS BECOME AN ARTIST OF ALL TRADES, LEARNING EVERYTHING THEY CAN TO FOLLOW THEIR DREAM. T'S PASSION FOR ART HAS LED THEM TO WORKING ON VIDEO GAMES, COSTUMES, AND NOW COMIC BOOKS!

than a power plant, bashing out gut-busting drum solos that blast away those bad days and set your heart ablaze!

Next, we have Tommy Goodtime, bearer of the bass and bringer of the rhythm. His name tells you all you need to know. Feel the thump of his bombastic basslines and before you know it, the worst of times become the best of times.

And, finally, holding the band together, we

 have Florence Banshee. Known as Flo to her friends, Florence Banshee is a down-to-earth singer of stories with a voice that is out of this world, bound to get your blood bubbling every time.

    Together, this fresh-out-of-water trio of rock 'n rolling oddballs are the Ooze Crew, champions of the power of the Ooze and ready to conquer the musical world.

Ooze Crew,

Ooze Crew,

Coming for you,

Feel the power,

The power of the Ooze!

CHAPTER 2

TRUTHFUL OR TRENDY? TAKE YOUR PICK

"Ready for tonight, gang?" Ricky Ignition excitedly tapped the tips of his drumsticks against his knees, practising the beat he would bring to the stage later that evening. Heading to a gig in their trusty van that they lovingly referred to as 'the Bandwagon' always had the Ooze Crew buzzing. Especially Ricky. Ricky was always ready to rock! However, the frustrated groan from Florence Banshee made even Ricky pause.

"What's wrong, Flo?" Ricky asked.

"Lazlo's going to be there, right?" said Florence, pinching the bridge of her

nose.

"Yeah, he texted earlier. He wants to meet us there," said Ricky.

"That's what's wrong," said Florence. "Just thinking about dealing with him has already given me a headache."

"Which one is Lazlo, again?" Tommy Goodtime asked from behind the wheel of the Bandwagon. "Wait, wasn't he the guy who threw up in the alley because we played so loud?"

"No," said Florence, "he's the loser who wants to be our manager."

"Well, bring him on. We'll tell him where to go!" Ricky grinned, resuming the light little beat against his knees.

"Betcha I can make that guy puke again tonight!" said Tommy, pulling up to the venue.

"Gross, Tommy," Ricky laughed.

Florence said nothing. She was in no mood for jokes, and sure enough, the cause of her headaches soon came slinking around the corner.

"Hey, guys! Good to see you."

"Oh, brother," Florence groaned.

It was Lazlo. Lazlo was, without a doubt, a man of style. At least, on the surface. He was forever fitted out in a tailored suit, with a clean-shaven face and a crop of flawlessly combed bleach-blond hair. His overall appearance was quite impressive. However, it wasn't enough to fool the Ooze Crew. Especially Florence. Florence knew a bad egg when she smelled one.

"How's the Ooze Cruise doing?" Lazlo asked, approaching the band with a wave and a smile that was just a little too sugary to be sincere.

"It's 'Ooze Crew'," Florence corrected sternly.

"For now," said Lazlo with a dismissive shrug.

"Hey, look, it is puke guy!" said

Tommy as he and Ricky walked by, both snickering under their breath. Lazlo seemed utterly oblivious to their taunting and continued with his pre-prepared speech.

"I think Ooze Cruise will look much better on our future records. What do you think?"

"There's no 'our', Lazlo," said Florence, quickly getting heated. "We haven't signed any deal with you and we're never going to. What makes you think you can just boss us around?"

"I mean, I thought it was obvious,"

said Lazlo, looking irritatingly smug. "It's not that you guys are stupid – it's just that I'm much smarter than you. I mean, no offence, but  you lot don't really seem like the thinking type." Florence's blood began to boil. "Listen, Florence, I think you three could be the next big thing," Lazlo droned on. "You just need to change a few things. Nothing major. Just your clothes, your names and your music. You have to be more in with the current trends if you ever hope to get anywhere. I can help you with that. For a small fee, of course. Shall we say half the money the band makes? A 50/50 split? How does that sound?"

"It sounds like you should take your dumb face and—" Florence burst out. She looked ready to launch herself at Lazlo and she probably would have, had Tommy not hurriedly stepped between them.

"He's not worth it, Flo," Tommy interrupted, trying to calm her down. Ricky, meanwhile, threw Lazlo a stern glare. Ricky wasn't often stern, so when he was, you knew he meant it.

"Sorry, puke guy," said Ricky coldly. "We're not interested." Lazlo scowled and folded his arms.

"You artists and your mood swings," Lazlo sighed. "I can see the stage fright is getting to you. We'll talk later when you've all got your knickers in less of a twist."

"Oh, get real!" Florence snapped but was quickly stopped by Tommy again.

"Forget him, Flo. Let's just focus on the gig."

CHAPTER 3

GLORY VS. GREED

Hands clapped, feet tapped, and the crowd were unable to do anything else in the world but dance. The Ooze Crew had done it again. Their show was a roaring success. However, not everyone was celebrating.

Even though the fans felt the power of the Ooze, the same could not be said for Lazlo, who paced up and down in his office, scowling to himself as he debated what to do. This glory should have been his and those kids were stealing it from him.

"Those no-good punks!" he growled through gritted teeth. "Why won't they listen to me? I could be rich and famous if I could just make them do as I say!"

"Ah, another soul not getting what

they want," said a voice suddenly. It was deep and dark and filled the room. But there was no one in sight.

"Who said that?!" Lazlo gasped.

"Someone who can help," the voice whispered coldly over Lazlo's shoulder. "You want fame and fortune, am I correct?"

"Yes!" Lazlo replied, clutching his heart in desperation. "I want that more than anything. I want my name on the front cover of every hit record. I want wealth and fame. I want to rule the music business!"

"For that, you will need a band, won't you?" the voice asked.

"Yes, I just need a band to do what I say, and from there, I could build a musical empire. I could take over the world!"

A low chuckle rumbled in Lazlo's ears. "Take over the world, hm? Sounds exciting."

"Please," Lazlo begged, "you said you could help?"

"I can."

"Will you?"

The chuckle rose to a cackle. Lazlo felt a terrible jolt, as if he had just been electrocuted. He gasped in horror, and then he caught sight of his reflection in the window of his office. His eyes were glowing bright red. When the voice spoke again, it no longer echoed around the room nor settled upon his shoulder. This time, Lazlo heard it speak to him from inside his own head.

"Why not?" it rumbled.

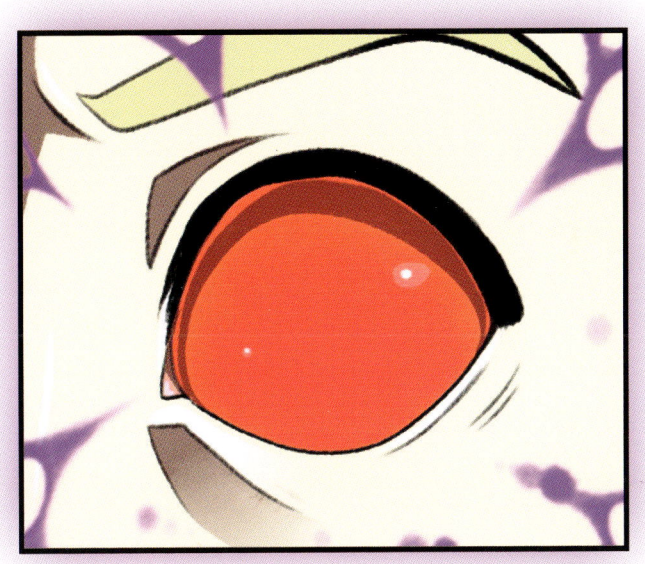

CHAPTER 4

OUT WITH A BANG!

Something struck the club. Something that could not be seen, only felt. It made the walls and floors quake and the entire crowd quiver. The band felt it, too. But it wasn't the power of the Ooze.

"I feel so funky," Ricky said, looking over to Tommy, who gave him a worried glance in return.

Florence, meanwhile, looked down at her microphone. Glimmers of red energy were buzzing around it like freakish flashes of lightning.

"What's happening?!" Her hair stood on end with every snap, crackle and pop. She only had to look at her equally bewildered bandmates and their now shimmering instruments to know that they were feeling it too.

"Guys!" she called out to the rest

of the band. But before anything could be done, the energy burst from their instruments like neon wires, bright red and boiling. It struck the ceilings, the floors and then the fuse box on the wall. With a flurry of sparks, everything went dark. Whatever that stuff was, it was strong enough to cut the power in the entire club!

"Everybody, stay calm!" Florence called, but she was drowned out by the audience, who were now screaming in alarm.

"Errr... Florence?" Tommy

said. Florence could hear the worry in his voice and she soon saw why. The fuse box had burst into flames. The flames were spreading... and they were spreading fast!

"Quick!" Florence yelled. "Get everybody out!"

CHAPTER 5

SAMUEL

"We were barely halfway through our set," Florence sighed.

"Well, at least nobody got hurt," said Ricky.

The entire club was now ablaze. Jets of water blasted through the flames as the firefighters helped the last of the stragglers to safety. The Ooze Crew, meanwhile, could do nothing but watch from a distance, utterly baffled by what had just occurred.

Tommy opened the back of the Bandwagon to get them all some water, only to become even more confused at what he saw.

"Uh... guys?" he called to the others. "Should our stuff still be doing that?"

Florence and Ricky looked around. It was their instruments. That bright electrical buzz was still there. Except now, it was constant. Their instruments were glowing like red-hot coals. Ricky picked up one of his drumsticks, cautiously at first. But they didn't burn his fingers like he expected them to. He raised an eyebrow thoughtfully.

"Do you think whatever blew the club's power did this to our instruments?"

"It sure did!"

Ricky started, letting out a squeak of surprise when he heard an unfamiliar voice. The Ooze Crew all turned in unison to see a man approaching. None of them recognised him but, unlike Lazlo, his face was kind. His large green eyes peered up at them from under the brim of a grey trilby hat, pulled down over a puff of white hair. He gave them all an airy wave

and a friendly smile.

"Hey there, Ooze Crew! How's it going? Sorry for scaring you there, youngblood."

"Scared? No, I'm all good," said Ricky, his tone just a little too high-pitched to be taken seriously.

"You sure about that, Ricky?" Tommy teased, prodding at Ricky, trying to make him jump again.

"I'm Samuel," said the man. "I'm a

big fan of your music."

"Thanks," said Florence. She took Ricky's other drumstick and held it up to show Samuel. "So, you know about whatever did this to our instruments?"

"I sure do," said Samuel with a wink. "I probably know more than anyone about what's got your instruments all in a funk."

"It's not dangerous, right?" Ricky asked worriedly.

"It depends how you use it," said Samuel. "Instruments like that have popped up all over the world. The same red glow, always appearing on nights like this. If played right, they can make some of the most beautiful music you've ever heard. If played wrong, they can do a lot of damage."

"Don't worry, Samuel. I know how to play my bass," said Tommy reassuringly.

"I don't think that's what he means, Tommy," Florence sighed.

"Not quite," Samuel replied. "I'm not just talking about playing the right notes, youngblood. If you play with heart, with love of the music, those instruments will make you sound amazing. But, if you just play looking for success, money and fame, these instruments will have a funny way of eating away at you."

"I hope that's just a figure of speech?" Tommy asked, a bit rattled by Samuel's wording.

Ricky, on the other hand, had already regained his usual spark. "Don't worry, Samuel," he said, proudly grasping his glowing drumsticks. "You can trust us to do the right thing! And you know what? We'll even prove it to you. We're playing at Fright Fest this weekend. You should

come on down!"

"I'll see you there, youngbloods!" said Samuel. "Now, I've got a bus to catch."

"Are you sure?" Ricky asked. "We could give you a ride?"

"I'm good," Samuel replied. "The old bus has never let me down." Samuel gave a wave and without another word,

 he disappeared around a corner and into a darkened alleyway.

"Samuel! Wait a sec!" Florence cried out, quickly following Samuel into the alley. But Samuel was nowhere to be seen. No one was there but them.

"Samuel?" Florence called.

"Oh, this just keeps getting weirder," Tommy added, shifting uncomfortably. Florence, meanwhile, stared down the empty alleyway.

"How did he do that...?"

CHAPTER 6

1922

WELCOME TO FRIGHT FEST! THE GNARLIEST EVENT THIS SUMMER

The Ooze Crew, all jammed into the Bandwagon, drove under the big banner signalling the venue of their next gig.

"Are you guys ready to rock this place?" Ricky asked, throwing his fist into the air in a burst of excitement.

"I'm pumped!" Tommy replied. "I can't wait to see how we sound now that all our stuff is magic."

"I don't remember Samuel saying

anything about magic, Tommy," said Ricky quizzically.

"Well, what else would make them glow like that?" Tommy said, turning to look back at Florence in the backseat. "What do you think, Flo?"

Florence didn't answer.

"Flo?"

Nothing.

She was staring at her phone, brows creased, and eyes narrowed. They had all been a little baffled after their mysterious meeting with Samuel and needed some time to get over the shock of what he had told them. While Ricky and Tommy were excited by this new information, Florence remained suspicious.

She hadn't been twiddling her thumbs since Samuel's disappearance. She had been doing some digging. As the Bandwagon approached the Fright Fest venue, she found herself staring at a black and white image on her phone, a picture she had stumbled across during her research into the glowing instruments and the mysterious Samuel.

The image was of an old-fashioned jazz player holding a trumpet. He looked just like the stranger in the alleyway. Underneath the photo was a name tag.

Samuel Golding, 1922

"What? This says 1922!" Florence burst out. "That can't be right!"

"Flo!"

Florence jumped and looked up to see Tommy, who was now trying to tug her out of the Bandwagon.

"C'mon, we're here! We need to get set up."

"Oh."

"Are you okay?" Tommy asked. "You've been quiet."

"Yeah, it's just—"

"Guys, c'mon," Ricky cut in, dragging out his drum kit piece by piece from the back of the Bandwagon. "We're

behind enough as it is. We need to get going!"

Florence shifted uneasily, before sliding her phone back into her pocket. "I'll tell you guys later. Let's just get this over with."

"Get it over with?" said Tommy. "That's not like you."

"Do you not think any of this is weird?"

"Well, yeah. But—"

"Hey, Ooze Crew!" They turned to see the Fright Fest manager standing at the backstage door, frantically waving the band in. "Hurry up, you're on next!"

"Like I said," Florence continued, grabbing her microphone, "I'll tell you guys after the show."

CHAPTER 7

THE GIG OF DOOM

Hands were clapping. Feet were tapping. The Fright Fest crowd flooded the edge of the stage, ready to feel the power of the Ooze!

"Ready to give these freaky instruments a go?" Tommy cheered, giving his bass a last-minute tune.

"Try and stop me!" Ricky replied from behind his drum kit, snatching up the sticks excitedly.

Florence took her usual place at centre stage, gripping her glowing microphone.

"That Samuel guy better be right about these things," she mused, before hiding her apprehension beneath her usual rock 'n' roll bravado.

"Hello, Fright Fest!" she bellowed into the mic. The crowd yelled back in an enthusiastic buzz. "We are the Ooze Crew, and we're here to amaze you! One, two, three, f—"

But before Florence could even finish counting in the first song, she was cut off by a scream from within the crowd. Except this wasn't a scream of excitement or anticipation. It was a terrible, blood-curdling scream, so shocking that the rest of the crowd parted, bringing into view a face that was all too familiar to the bewildered Ooze Crew.

"Lazlo?!" Florence burst out. It was indeed Lazlo, although he seemed quite different from his prim and proper self.

He looked dishevelled and deranged; his lips stretched into a maniacal grin that would make the hair of even the bravest soul stand on end.

"Well, if it isn't the Ooze Crew," Lazlo sneered. "Here to play more of your garbage music, hm?"

"What's wrong with his eyes?!" said Ricky, utterly horrified. They were glowing bright red, just like the instruments.

"We could have taken over the world together,"

Lazlo continued, his grin dropping to a venomous glare of vengeance, "if only you had listened to me. We could have had fame and riches beyond anything your pea brains could possibly imagine. Well, you missed your chance. Now, I'll just have to take over the world with a new band!"

"Who would want to start a band with you?" Florence retorted. "You're selfish and mean and arrogant!"

"Is that so? Then I'll just have to make one, won't I?"

"Wow. Puke guy's really gone this

time..." Tommy mumbled, unimpressed. Lazlo threw up his hands and cackled loudly, his gleaming red eyes as wide as saucers.

"Ladies and gentlemen," he yelled, "allow me to introduce to you the hit new band, all the way from another world!" No sooner had the words left his lips than the ground began to split. From the cracks seeped a pulsing gunge in a gross mixture of green, blue and red. It crawled and wriggled as if it were alive before splitting into three. Each pile of goop grew to a colossal size until they towered far above even the tallest person in the room, almost reaching the ceiling. "THE OOZE CRUISE," Lazlo bellowed triumphantly, standing before his hideous creation.

The blue oozing figure on the left sat in front of a twisted mound shaped

vaguely like a drum kit, while the green figure on the right held something that looked like a bass guitar, and the red figure in the middle clutched a dripping, misshapen microphone.

As Lazlo roared his introduction, this bizarrely monstrous band let out a deafening screech.

The Ooze Crew covered their ears, left dumbfounded on the stage while all those who hadn't already fled for their lives now turned tail and ran.

"They sound terrible!" Florence growled through gritted teeth.

"And they totally ripped off our name," Ricky added, a little more than miffed.

"We don't sound like that, do we?" Tommy asked.

"Not at all," said a gentle voice from behind the band. The Ooze Crew turned to see a familiar face.

"Samuel!"

"Looks like you've got some work to do," said Samuel, looking concerned.

"What are we supposed to do?!" said Florence.

"Well, you can't let Lazlo get away with this," said Samuel.

"How, though?" Florence asked desperately. Samuel turned to look at the three freakish figures. He didn't seem angry, or annoyed, or irritated. Just a little bit sad.

"Listen, youngblood," he said calmly, "Lazlo is wrong. Music isn't for getting rich and famous. It's for expressing yourself and making your own art. The bravest thing a musician can do is play how they want, no matter what anyone says!"

The Ooze Crew exchanged glances and with sudden determination, Florence narrowed her eyes.

"Samuel's right," she said. "It's time to show Lazlo what the

Ooze Crew are all about!"

Ricky and Tommy both threw up their hands, sharing in their bandmate's newfound fire.

"Yeah!"

"Let's send these monsters home!"

"Tommy! Hit 'em with that bassline," said Florence.

Tommy Goodtime snatched up his

bass and grinned. "With pleasure!"

"Now, Ricky! Drum as hard as you can!"

"Don't have to tell me twice, Flo!" Ricky Ignition was already on it, bashing out a gunge-busting drum solo to the beat of Tommy Goodtime's bombastic bassline. Their glowing instruments lit up as if they were on fire. The ground quaked and the

monsters quivered.

Florence snatched up her microphone, grinning from ear to ear. "This is it," she murmured. She raised the microphone to her lips and bellowed out the slime-melting chorus of their signature song.

Ooze Crew,

Ooze Crew,

Coming for you,

Feel the power,

The power of the Ooze!

CHAPTER 8

OOZING WITH INNER FIRE

Even with so much at stake, the band was beaming. They had music in them that only they could play. It was theirs and no one else could change that. That feeling, that love of the music, set their instruments ablaze. It was the power of the Ooze. It filled the room to the point of bursting.

For a moment, the creatures' screeching became louder, as if they were crying out in defeat. Sure enough, as Florence's voice filled the room, the monstrous copycat band began to twist and contort, before exploding into formless piles of rancid gunge.

"No!" Lazlo cried, clutching fistfuls of his hair in a state of utter despair. "My monsters! My band! My fortune!"

The Ooze Cruise was no more.

"We did it!" the Ooze Crew yelled.

"You two are the best bandmates in the world!" Ricky added, slinging his arms around his two buddies.

Florence faltered.

"Hang on," she said. "Did anyone see where Samuel went?"

The rest of the band paused, taking a moment to look around. Florence was right. Samuel was nowhere to be seen. Tommy scratched his head, clearly baffled. Ricky simply shrugged.

"I guess he must have had another bus to catch," he said. But they were soon distracted by another sound. A very familiar sound, at that.

"Do you hear that?" said Tommy.

It was the whooping and cheering of an eager audience.

"The crowd's back!" said Ricky.

Florence smirked, picking up her microphone. "Sounds like they want an encore," she said. As she counted in her bandmates with a one, a two, a three and a four, hands started clapping, feet started tapping and the crowd could do nothing else in the world but dance.

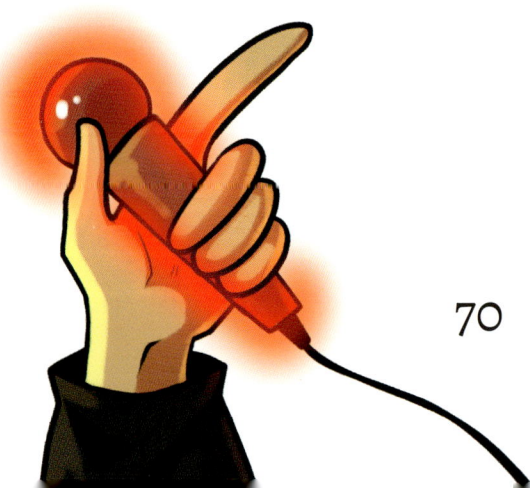

Ooze Crew,

Ooze Crew,

Coming for you,

Feel the power,

The power of the Ooze!

Lazlo, meanwhile, his eyes ablaze with that same fiery glow, slunk away, unacknowledged and unnoticed...

THE END

The Ooze Crew are the coolest band on the block and they're about to hit it big time!

Everyone has music inside them in one form or another and the Ooze Crew are all too happy to share theirs with the world. However, there are those who are looking to snap up a piece of the Ooze for all the wrong reasons. From sneaky managers to mysterious musicians, they have got quite the ride ahead of them...